CHINOOK COUNTRY
Alberta South

CHINOOK COUNTRY
Alberta South

Photographs by Bill Simpkins

Introduction by Grant MacEwan
Foreword by Peter Lougheed

Toronto
OXFORD UNIVERSITY PRESS
1979

I would like to dedicate this book to the people of Southern Alberta and in doing so I would also like to thank all those who have helped in producing the book, especially my friends at the Calgary Herald *for allowing me to use some of their material, and for their continued, unfailing support.*

BILL SIMPKINS

Designed by FORTUNATO AGLIALORO

© Oxford University Press (Canadian Branch) 1979
2 3 4-2 1
Printed in Hong Kong by
EVERBEST PRINTING COMPANY LIMITED

Foreword

Whether through the printed word or the camera eye, it is important that citizens of Alberta and other Canadians have the opportunity to become more familiar with their surroundings.

The collection of photographs in this book exhibits the history and beauty that is abundant in Alberta.

To capture the spirit of Southern Alberta was not an easy task for Bill Simpkins—but I know the gallery of pictures between these covers exhibits that ever-present spirit found in this part of Alberta.

PETER LOUGHEED
Premier of the Province of Alberta

2   3

Introduction
by Grant MacEwan

Alberta South is a land of bewitching contrasts. Nature created it that way and a generation of newcomers added substantially to it. The result of the new intervention was not all good and not all bad, but it was spectacular. Who saw it more clearly than my wise old friend, the Old Man of the Stoney Tribe who was born beside the Bow River and died beside the Bow 96 years later, while Canada was marking the centennial of Confederation?

His life embraced the Old and the New; he had been permitted to see and know the best and worst of two worlds. In the lowly circumstances of boyhood he saw no vehicle more serviceable and luxurious than a travois—consisting simply of two slender lodgepole pine sticks dragging behind a dog or horse. Then, amazingly, he lived to view the bigger world from a high-speed jet plane, actually encircling it. As a man from the teepees in the Land of the Unusual, he was adding to the contrasts by declaring for the principles of understanding and brotherhood and facing bigger total audiences than any other ambassador who ever went from Canada.

Still he could remember when the territory encompassed by this book was buffalo country, when missionary John McDougall could stand on Spy Hill—now within the bounds of a great city—and see what he believed to be half a million 'wild bison critters'. The social order then was presided over by five buffalo-hunting tribes of native people: Blackfoot, Blood, Piegan, Sarcee, and his own, the Stoney. Their reputation was for ferocity, and they were the last of the Prairie tribesmen to enter into a treaty with the Government of Canada.

They were primitive people, but their stewardship over thousands of years and millions of acres was good. The native herds and flocks were undiminished; the scenery remained unspoiled as the Great Spirit had fashioned it; the soil and grass and forests suffered no depletion; the coal and oil and gas were not ravaged; stream water retained its sparkling clearness and the atmosphere over the Bow was unblotched by gaseous smogs. Nature was in a state of enduring harmony.

But it did not take the members of the new race long to change things. As a witness, the Old Man from the teepees was saddened at the scars left by the new human tenants. With a mild rebuke, he said he was thankful that the Rocky Mountains, the blue sky, the eroded Badlands, the Prairie vistas, and the returning moisture that sent vegetation into spirals of new growth each spring were beyond the greedy and destructive grasp of white men.

He made no pretense of knowing history, but having known the stalwart leaders of two races who brought personality to the Southwest, he knew more of southern Alberta history than he realized. He could tell about the great Indians: Red Crow, Yellow Horn, Bullhead, Bearspaw, and Crowfoot, who was hailed as Chief of Chiefs. He knew the qualities of muscle, mind, and courage they possessed, entitling them to be remembered as great Albertans.

He recalled, too, the white man's 'Chiefs' who helped to make the area distinctive: the pioneer statesman, Frederick Haultain, who was the perennial Premier of the North West Territories before 1905; Dr Michael Clark, who sat for Red Deer in the House of Commons and was regarded as the best orator in Canada at a time when oratory was in fashion; and R.B. Bennett, with whom the Indians had business dealings and who became the Prime Minister of Canada.

The Old Man—a sort of symbol of the Southwest—could recall attending school at Red Deer when it was still known as The Crossing. He travelled with his people along the southern rivers when Fort Macleod was nothing more than a police post and Lethbridge was known as Coalbanks, and he attended Calgary's first fair, the ancestor of a world-famous Exhibition and Stampede, in 1886. He preferred these places when they possessed a charm of childhood, before they were caught up in thrusts for growth and quests for wealth.

He saw in sorrow the city perimeters becoming areas of conflict between those who wanted expansion and growth at any price and those who, like himself, believed that productive soil should be safeguarded for its most natural purposes.

But the same native patriarch conceded that the changes made by white men were not all bad. Banff and Lake Louise had been allowed to keep their natural glory. The forest watershed of the Foothills was given protection. Glenmore, the man-made lake in Calgary, would have had full Indian approval as one of the richest gems in the crown of southern Alberta treasures.

The Old Man was well aware that the Rockies had won millions of hearts and that highways leading to Banff are busy around the year. But he knew, also, that people sometimes overlook Nature's goodness found in other directions. Driving the highway from Red Deer to Waterton Lakes is like following a dividing line separating the grassy Foothills, which offer perpetual grazing, from the ocean-like expanses of Prairie. And what too often escapes proper appreciation is that apparently limitless patchwork of farms that stretches to Drumheller, yes and to Regina and Winnipeg.

When travellers of today, like the Indians of yesterday, wander deep into the plains they reach the shortgrass ranges, and then the Cypress Hills. Rising from the plain to 4,000 feet above sea level, as if to assert lordship over the surroundings, these hills boast different rainfall, different flora, different fauna. Captain John Palliser in 1859 saw them as an 'oasis' in the vast expanse of dry prairie.

Or penetrating the Prairies northward, the traveller encounters the Red Deer River Badlands, sufficiently weird and wonderful to be almost unbelievable. Chiselled by millions of years of erosion, the display of shapes and scenes seems to belong to fairyland or an abode of goblins.

Amid the diversity of Nature's wonders, it should not be surprising that southern Alberta attracted or created so many of the most colourful personalities – both Indians and Whites – in frontier history. They blended with the heritage.

Alberta South has come to be seen as an area of rare photographic resources. They are resources, happily, that can be exploited without depletion. Now it is gratifying that the challenge of capturing an important part of the story of the South in pictures has been recognized and grasped by one who is both able and eager to discharge the task. My old friend of the Stonies would have approved. All success to Bill Simpkins. May his imagination and his camera eye never fail him.

7 Indian Village, Calgary Exhibition and Stampede
8 Indian Village, Calgary Exhibition and Stampede

9   Indian Days, near Stand-Off
10 Watching Chicken Dancers at Calgary Exhibition and Stampede

11 Drumheller Exhibition and Stampede, Drumheller
12 North of Rosebud

15   16

19 Jumping Pound
20 Lundbreck area

21 Simon's Valley area
22 near Carbon

23   Sugar-beets, Taber

24   Hutterites, Beiseker

25 Blairmore
26 Stettler County Fair, Stettler

27 Gleichen

28   Market, Calgary

29   30

32   Wildhorse

33 Writing-on-Stone Provincial Park and Sweetgrass Hills
34 Weaselhead area, Glenmore Dam, Calgary

35 Cattledrive, Bow Crow Forest Reserve
36 Round-up, Lone Star Ranch, Jumping Pound

37 Cowboy, Lone Star Ranch
38 Cowboy's gear, Lone Star Ranch

39 Chuckwagon race, Calgary
Exhibition and Stampede
40 Bareback event, Calgary
Exhibition and Stampede

41 Calf-roping event, Calgary Exhibition and Stampede
42 Drumheller Exhibition and Stampede, Drumheller

43 Rig workers, Crossfield

44 Longview

45 Cochrane
46 Horse-head well-pump near Longview

47 Langdon Corner

48   Heritage Park, Calgary

49 Foremost

51 Firehall, Lethbridge
52 Saint Patrick's Roman Catholic
Church, Medicine Hat

53 Kananaskis Country
54 Alberta Rose, Hartell

58   Millarville

59 Bow Lake

60 Lake Louise Creek
61 Exshaw

62   CPR Station, Banff

63 Banff Avenue, Banff

64   Banff Springs Hotel, Banff
65   Banff Springs Hotel, Banff

70   Richmond Road, Calgary
71   near Priddis

72   Elk, Eisenhower Junction, Banff National Park
73   Canmore

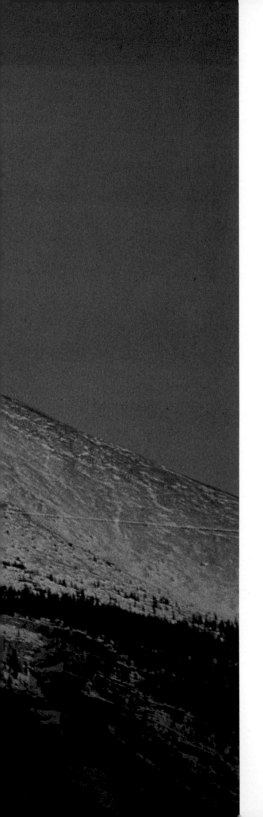
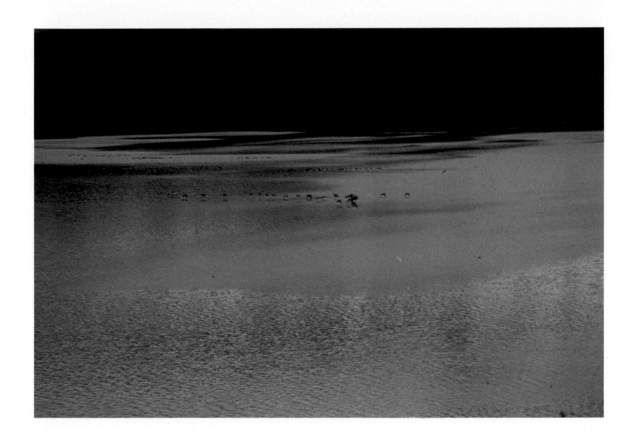

74 Canmore
75 Glenmore Dam, Calgary

76 Prince of Wales Hotel, Waterton
77 Fishermen on Cameron Lake

78 Hoary Marmot, Dolomite Pass
79 Road to Rosebud, Lebanon School

81 East Coulee

82 Cypress Hills Provincial Park

◁ 80 Monarch

83 Consolation Lakes

84 85 86   Dinosaur Provincial Park, Brooks

◁87 Suffield
88 Chinook 'arch', Calgary